Contents

Executive Summary

It has long been recognized that the new state of South Sudan would face daunting challenges. The world's newest nation is also one of its poorest—the result of negligible investment in its people and infrastructure over many decades by the erstwhile governing authority in Khartoum. War ravaged the country nearly continuously since 1955, costing over 2 million lives. South Sudan's state-building effort, moreover, started from a rudimentary institutional base, having inherited few functional governance systems. What governance structures existed were confined to former garrison towns such as Juba, the capital, in a territory roughly equivalent to Afghanistan with a population of 11.8 million people. Adding to the difficulty is the very real risk of renewed conflict with Sudan and the chicanery on the part of the government there to stir up trouble in its southern neighbor. In short, South Sudan was bound to face struggles.

Despite the steep road South Sudan must climb, the performance of the Government of the Republic of South Sudan (RSS) since independence in July 2011 has made it steeper still, disappointing citizens and international partners alike. President Salva Kiir himself has decried the diversion of public monies—perhaps as much as $4 billion—by leading government and military officials. Perceptions are widespread of senior government malfeasance, self-interest, and disregard for citizen priorities. Meanwhile, state authority remains heavily centralized within the executive branch, where decisions are often made opaquely and without consultation or oversight. This has been matched by regular reports of repression by the army and the police, conveying an impression that government officials see their role as one of self-enrichment and maintaining power rather than provision of services to citizens.

Ethnic divisions, long exploited by Khartoum during the war, have been deepened by the perception of Dinka dominance of the RSS. These fears have been reinforced by dubious state and national elections in 2010 that favored candidates from the Sudan People's Liberation Movement. In some cases, this has translated into open insurgency followed by brutal reprisals by the Sudan People's Liberation Army. Hundreds of innocent civilians have been killed in the process, particularly in Jonglei state but also in pockets of rising insecurity around the country.

The new country is not without assets. It took control of developed oil fields that are estimated to yield 350,000 barrels per day and annual net oil export revenues (at full potential) of roughly $9 billion for the government. The population in South Sudan, furthermore, is nothing if not resilient, having endured years of hardship, isolation, and war. Much of the expansive territory is highly fertile for agricultural production, though only 4 percent is currently under cultivation. Moreover, South Sudan enjoys a font of international good will, with key partners in East Africa, Europe, and the United States having provided extensive humanitarian assistance to South Sudan throughout the war and overwhelmingly endorsed the new state's quest for independence and membership at the United Nations.

Efforts to meet the young state's many challenges will fail, however, without greater trust and social cohesion between the new government and citizens. State-society relations provide the foundation for any state. If this foundation is strong, built on the principles of trust and legitimacy, then even poor countries can be stable and withstand intense external threats. Conversely, if the foundation is weak, then instability will persist irrespective of government revenue flows, the strength of the security sector, or the maneuvers of any external adversary. Strengthening state-society relations, then, is an imperative for the state-building and stabilization agenda of South Sudan.

In some cases, though, the government is directly undermining this confidence by inhibiting the emergence of accountability processes. This is the case, for instance, when the RSS constrains access to independent information through the media and civil society. Intimidation and outright attacks on journalists and human rights advocates are antithetical to building an inclusive, accountable state. Even more troubling, government actions to vilify ethnic communities home to rebel militia groups—such as the Murle population in Jonglei state—and failure to hold security services accountable for attacks on civilians, destroy social cohesion across communities and prevent trust in the state.

To improve state-society relations in the near term, the government must cease actions that alienate society from the state and focus on three critical tasks: building inclusive coalitions to support key institutional reforms, protecting space for independent voices in order to foster a national dialogue over the priorities for the new state, and achieving some tangible development progress to demonstrate the government's responsiveness to citizen expectations. While South Sudan has suffered serious setbacks in its quest for state legitimacy during its first years of independence, upcoming foundational state-building processes afford opportunities for the government to reverse the deterioration: the national constitution review process, the national reconciliation process, the 2015 elections, and investment in public infrastructure that will link disparate regions of the new nation. Central to each will be a massive civic education campaign to inform and invite participation from all parts of South Sudanese society in a national dialogue on citizen expectations of the state and what it means to be South Sudanese.

The foundation of the state cannot be an afterthought. It must come before the structure is built. Generating renewed confidence in state-society relations through these opportunities will provide the social capital needed to strengthen institutions most central to ending violence: citizen security (ensuring citizens' freedom from physical violence and from fear of violence), justice (providing recourse to nonviolent dispute resolution), and jobs (enabling livelihoods without recourse to violence). South Sudan's leadership can set a new course toward legitimacy, stability, and sustained development if it prioritizes building trust and social cohesion within the South Sudanese population.

The Challenge to Stability from State-Society Relations in South Sudan

The world's youngest state, South Sudan, faces numerous acute challenges. Unresolved disputes with Sudan over oil pipeline usage, the status of the disputed Abyei region, border demarcation, and allegations of support for proxy militia groups occasionally flare up into cross-border military clashes that generate international headlines and fuel predictions of renewed war between North and South.

Serious internal strains also abound. Intercommunal violence between South Sudan's many ethnic groups poses a deadly and complex challenge to the new country's stability and coherence. While not a new phenomenon, the frequency and intensity of ethnic violence in South Sudan has been on the rise since 2009 with thousands killed.[1] For some communities, it is so intense and localized that neither the end of the civil war nor independence has apparently made an appreciable difference in their daily security.[2]

Government security responses have, at times, inflamed ethnic tensions and contributed to escalating the violence rather than lessening it. Security operations by the Sudan People's Liberation Army (SPLA) primarily consist of coercive civilian disarmament campaigns after intercommunal violence flares. The campaigns have achieved only marginal success and been followed by immediate rearmament of the communities in question, particularly since the campaigns typically proceed sequentially, leaving newly disarmed communities vulnerable to attack from their as-yet disarmed neighbors. Serious human rights abuses by SPLA soldiers and South Sudan National Police Service officers against the communities being disarmed have further negated any security gains from these campaigns.[3] In 2013, government security responses to an insurgency in Jonglei state collided with intercommunal violence between several ethnic groups, resulting in the displacement of tens of thousands of people, serious humanitarian distress, reports of killings and torture, and other allegations of gross human rights abuses by forces on all sides, notably the government.[4]

Predation and repression by government security forces is not the only self-inflicted wound causing internal stress and eroding citizens' trust in the government. Perceptions of widespread corruption and government disinterest in citizens' expectations are strong. Fifty-nine percent of South Sudanese believe government corruption is worsening and 75 percent are dissatisfied with the government's efforts to fight corruption.[5] These views are reinforced by disappointment with the slow pace of development progress, made more acute by inflation, which has soared since independence, significantly increasing the cost of living for all South Sudanese. Hikes in food prices have hit especially hard given the limited levels of local food production, high reliance on imported food, and Sudan's prohibition on cross-border trade with South Sudan since independence.

Limits on freedom of expression and access to independent information have risen since independence in 2011. South Sudan was declared "Not Free" and barely edged out Zimbabwe in the quality of its political rights and civil liberties in its first appearance on the annual Freedom in the World assessment by Freedom House. Journalists who write about corruption and other governement abuses are frequently subject to harassment and attacks. Coupled with South Sudan's extremely low socioeconomic development, large youth bulge, landlocked geography, war-ridden past, and a generally unstable regional neighborhood, the prospects for reverting back to conflict, this time internal, are formidable.

Underlying all these challenges, however, is the weakness of the foundation on which the legitimacy of the new state of South Sudan rests: its state-society relations. Ultimately, these relations will determine the country's stability and even viability. As a new state, South Sudan has few of the institutional checks and balances—such as electoral management bodies, legislatures, courts, political parties, subnational government offices, a merit-based civil service, a professional security sector, an independent media, and civil society—through which state-society relations are productively managed and stresses absorbed. The country's constitution, for example, should enshrine the agreed upon rules for how state and society will relate. However, South Sudan still lacks a permanent constitution forged through a broad-based, inclusive, public dialogue and subjected to popular referendum for approval.

Understandably, such institutions of accountability take time to develop and therefore are in various states of functionality in South Sudan. Less understandably are government actions that undermine confidence in the state through its own limited and often overbearing engagement with citizens. At times, this entails the active marginalization of ethnic communities home to rebel militia groups. Failure to hold security services accountable for attacks on civilians also destroys trust across communities and in the government itself, further perpetuating the stunting of state-society relations.

A window of opportunity is closing for South Sudan. Participation in the referendum on independence was tremendous—more than 75 percent of the eligible population registered to vote, and 98 percent of those who cast ballots opted for independence. South Sudanese were overwhelmingly unified on this issue. However, such unity is fraying under the weight of perceived autocratic tendencies of the government, disregard for public opinion, and ethnic bias.

The growing potential for instability in South Sudan also has significant implications for the region. During the civil war, 4 million South Sudanese were displaced internally while some 628,000 fled across borders, stretching the capabilities and finances of neighboring states. The prospect of renewed turmoil in South Sudan could lead to similar levels of spillover and further regional instability. South Sudan also borders the Central African Republic and the Democratic Republic of the Congo, where rebel groups roam across borders freely. The Lord's Resistance Army (LRA) has frequently used South Sudan as a sanctuary.

The international community has invested billions of dollars over the years to address humanitarian needs and forge peace in the Sudans. Considerable diplomacy is still focused on outstanding disputes with Khartoum. Yet gains in stabilizing this vast region are most vulnerable to South Sudan's unaddressed internal weaknesses. It is the challenge of strengthening state-society relations that will determine whether South Sudan breaks free from recurrent cycles of violence and finds its footing as a stable, resilient state. Without greater trust and social cohesion between the new government and citizens, efforts to meet the current political, security, economic, and social crises confronting the young state will fail.

Ethnic Violence in Jonglei State

Ethnic fault lines abound in South Sudan (see Figure 1). The most persistent and pernicious conflicts are between the Dinka, Nuer, and Shilluk ethnic groups in Upper Nile state; the Lou and Jikany Nuer in Upper Nile and Jonglei states; and the Murle, Lou Nuer, and Dinka in Jonglei state. Ethnic conflict also frequently arises at the intersection of Unity, Lakes, and Warrap states. Frayed ethnic relations in other states occasionally erupt into violent confrontation, such as between the Dinka and Fertit in Western Bahr el Ghazal state, or between Equatorians and Dinka in and around Juba. While some have their roots in competition over resources (land, water, and cattle), others arise from legacies of political competition between southern leaders during the war or from disgruntled aspiring political leaders.

Jonglei has become the epicenter of the most deadly ethnic violence in South Sudan, with the single worst incident taking place between December 2011 and January 2012, when some 8,000 Lou Nuer youth raided Murle communities killing at least 1,000, displacing more than 100,000, and stealing 100,000 head of cattle.[6] The assault is part of a downward spiral of Lou Nuer-Murle attacks and reprisals that began in 2009. Government interventions to stop mass violence can best be described as too little and too late, including a wholly unsuccessful attempt to prevent the January 2012 attack. Some have accused the government of aiding the Lou Nuer militias.

This cycle of revenge attacks was further compounded by the reemergence of militia leader David Yau Yau in mid-2012. Yau Yau lost a 2010 election for a Jonglei state assembly seat to a candidate from the ruling SPLM party. Yau Yau subsequently took up arms, some of which have been traced back to Khartoum, and may command as many as 4,000-6,000 combatants, though many are only loosely affiliated to his rebellion. In March 2013, the SPLA launched a brutal counterinsurgency campaign against Yau Yau's forces and associated Murle youth, resulting in a dire humanitarian situation for more than 120,000 people by mid-2013 as well as allegations of gross human rights abuses against civilians. The United Nations Mission to South Sudan (UNMISS) has also been caught in the crossfire with the downing of one of its helicopters by the SPLA and a vicious attack killing five peacekeepers and seven civilians by Yau Yau's militia. According to the Small Arms Survey, many Murle no longer identify the Lou Nuer as their principal enemy, but rather the SPLA, state and national governments, and by extension the Dinka community.

Such intercommunal tensions and counterproductive responses by the government perpetuate and deepen conflict dynamics within South Sudan, severely limiting prospects for productive relations among ethnic groups and between the government and communities. Rebel militia leaders continue to trade on these grievances to mobilize youths against the state and other ethnic communities. Thus, not only does the government response fail to protect citizens, its actions can directly exacerbate perceptions of marginalization and discrimination.

South Sudan's Path to Statehood

South Sudan's present inability to provide security or services for its people frequently leads to the conclusion that it is a failed state. This presupposes that it was at some point a functioning state. Yet, South Sudan's only modern governance model has been the predatory, repressive, and sectarian rule of successive regimes in Khartoum.

Even among Sub-Saharan Africa's many weak states, the shallowness of South Sudan's government capacity and institutional depth make it an outlier. With a mere 6 years of experience as an autonomous regional government within Sudan from 2005 to 2011, South Sudan became the world's newest independent state on July 9, 2011. Prior to this, southern Sudan was mired in civil war with the Government of Sudan (GOS) from 1955 to 1972 and again from 1983 to 2005. Between 1972 and 1983, a semiautonomous regional government nominally ruled the South. In reality, the central government in Khartoum provided it few resources.

Britain's indirect colonial rule (1899-1955) effectively separated southern Sudan from northern Sudanese and Egyptian rule, leaving it to "develop" indigenously, with minimal administrative presence, no infrastructure, and nominal support to missionary churches to provide limited schooling and medical services. It took the British well into the 1920s to even pacify the South. It finally did so largely through stabilizing the tribal system, not through any centralized governance. Unlike the North, which had a history of centralized governance to draw on from Turco-Egyptian and Mahdist rule, the South had no such experience, rendering indirect rule all the more attractive for Britain. Rather, existing authority structures were highly differentiated across the South's 62 main ethnic groups (over 90 if subgroups are counted). Traditions of customary laws, courts, and conflict resolution within and between tribes varied greatly. What social norms of collective action that did exist centered on the tribe. Some had cultures of holding chiefs accountable to their people. Others did not. Where these norms existed, they were eroded by decades of civil war. Anchors of cultural unity, such as the predominance of Islam and Arabic in the North, were absent in southern Sudan.[7]

After World War II, Britain decided that southern Sudan should be administered from Khartoum and not integrated into British East Africa, as previously planned. The replacement of British district commissioners with northerners precipitated the outbreak of the first civil war between North and South in 1955, even before independence was granted to Sudan on January 1, 1956. The regime in Khartoum sent administrators to key provincial towns, but their authority never extended to the rural areas where the majority of the population lived. Even during the 1972-1983 break in fighting, the semiautonomous southern regional government struggled to effect governance beyond municipal boundaries.

For much of the second civil war (1983-2005), southern rebel factions, predominantly the Sudan People's Liberation Movement/ Army (SPLM/A) led by Dr. John Garang, held the majority of the territory of southern Sudan. The GOS in Khartoum retained control of key provincial capitals, including the capital of the South, Juba. Fierce competition between southern military and political leaders over liberation strategies, stoked to a considerable degree by Khartoum's malevolent intervention and manipulation, played out in atrocities and reprisals across ethnic groups and subgroups that cost more civilian lives than direct warfare between northern and southern forces. This left deep fault lines that have yet to be redressed in any meaningful reconciliation process.

Significantly, the two bitterest southern rivals, John Garang and Riek Machar, did not reconcile until 2003, midway through the negotiation of the Comprehensive Peace Agreement (CPA) with Khartoum that ultimately ended the war. This alliance, along with the incorporation of other southern rebel groups into the SPLM/A, ultimately enabled the people of southern Sudan to unite behind the CPA as the best hope for ending the war and achieving their objective of autonomous rule.

During the war, the southern rebel movements largely relied upon—and often extracted forcefully—support from the civilian population. A massive humanitarian operation, largely coordinated by the United Nations and comprising a wide array of international nongovernmental organizations and local churches, provided the only services that reached southern Sudanese civilians. Cycles of flooding and drought coupled with denial of humanitarian access by the GOS produced severe humanitarian crises and famine. Populations close to the North-South divide were subjected to forced displacement, slavery, and cattle raiding by northern militias. The LRA in northern Uganda conducted regular attacks and kidnappings among communities in the far southern states. Throughout the South, civilians feared bombing raids by Khartoum and being caught in the crossfire of South-South infighting, the nastiest incidents of which tapped into the fears and rivalries between the Dinka and Nuer communities. It is estimated that over 2 million southern Sudanese died and over 4.6 million were displaced during the second civil war.[8] This is out of an estimated population of 8.3 million people at the end of the war.

When it was established in July 2005, the interim Government of Southern Sudan (GoSS) started building nearly all institutions and administrative structures of government from scratch. It was not even in possession of its capital city, Juba, until after the untimely death of John Garang 3 weeks after taking office as President of Southern Sudan and First Vice President of Sudan. Six years later, now under the independent government of the Republic of South Sudan (RSS), the new country (with significant international support) had erected the basic elements of a modern state, including a transitional constitution, an executive office, a legislative assembly, a judicial system, and an army and police force.

Not surprisingly, South Sudan's development indicators are among the worst in the world. According to 2013 estimates, 51 percent of South Sudan's 11.8 million citizens are below the age of 18. This includes an estimated 2.3 million southern Sudanese displaced during the civil war who have returned to their communities since 2005. Of those 15 years and older, only 27 percent (40 percent male, 16 percent female) can read and write. Infant mortality stands at 70 per 1,000 live births, the 18th worst in the world. The fertility rate is 5.5 children per woman, the 9th highest globally. In a territory approximately the size of Afghanistan, it has only one paved highway running roughly 120 miles from Juba to the Ugandan border.

This history combined with a very small educated class, minimal physical infrastructure, marginal economic activity outside of subsistence agriculture and pastoralism, and an absence of social services create monumental challenges for improving living conditions.

Declining Confidence in Government

Even though South Sudan possesses extremely limited state capacity, the SPLM enjoys inherent legitimacy stemming from its experience fighting Africa's longest civil war and winning independence for its people. Nearly 99 percent of South Sudanese voters opted for independence in a referendum in January 2011. Popular support for and pride in the new nation was at its highest on South Sudan's Independence Day, July 9, 2011. The international community lent further legitimacy through its embrace of South Sudan as a sovereign state and the newest member of the United Nations and the African Union.

After decades of exploitation and neglect by Khartoum, expectations of the dividends of peace were high. Citizens believed their new government would deliver major improvements in development and security once the government was in full control of its national resources. Such hopes were augmented by expectations that the 6-year interim period of autonomy prior to the independence referendum would have allowed the new government sufficient time to plan and prepare. They expected to live in relative safety without fear of daily violence once freed from northern oppression.[9]

The government's post-independence honeymoon was fairly short-lived, however. Surveys indicated that by May 2013, half of all South

Sudanese felt the country was headed in the wrong direction. Top reasons cited for respondents' pessimism were heightened levels of insecurity, rising costs of living, and dissatisfaction with the pace of development, with particularly elevated concerns over food shortages and poverty (see Figure 2).[10]

To some extent, such attitudes are an inevitable outcome of the young state's extremely limited capacity measured against the severity of its challenges. Nevertheless, popular perceptions of willful government negligence (corruption, human rights abuses by the security services, closing of political space) and disinterest in meeting critical security, justice, and development expectations contribute to negative state-society dynamics that challenge the confidence of citizens in their state. Tellingly, perceptions of poor service delivery and government corruption have grown markedly worse since independence. This dissatisfaction with and decline in trust of the government poses one of the greatest state-building challenges to the new nation (see Figure 3).

Debilitating Corruption

South Sudanese perceive the ruling elite as overwhelmingly corrupt, in part because of the view that there has been little development despite 6 years of oil revenues since the GoSS was formed in 2005. In June 2012, President Kiir issued a public letter to 75 incumbent or former government officials and military officers, stating that $4 billion in government resources was missing. He demanded that the money be returned or else prosecutions would be launched. "We fought for freedom, justice and equality. Many of our friends died to achieve these objectives. Yet, once we got to power, we forgot what we fought for and began to enrich ourselves at the expense of our people," wrote President Kiir. "The credibility of our government is on the line."

While stunningly candid, the letter remains highly controversial—the figure has yet to be substantiated, and, thus far, no senior official has been prosecuted for corruption. (In June 2013, two ministers were suspended pending an investigation into a controversial procurement.) The impression left is of a ruling elite that enjoys total impunity, generating a sense of betrayal and anger for a lack of accountability for corruption. It also reinforces the exclusionary grievances of ethnic groups who feel less well represented in the government and military (which are largely dominated by the Dinka and Nuer) and therefore excluded from the spoils.

State institutions such as the Anti-Corruption Commission and the Office of the Auditor General are only just beginning to operate. Senior government officials filed asset disclosures with the Anti-Corruption Commission for the first time in 2012. The Auditor General is systematically reviewing the finances of the GoSS (prior to independence) and submitting regular public reports of his findings to the National Legislative Assembly with recommendations for further investigations. These measures are an important start in confronting the challenge of corruption and restoring confidence in public office holders. Until individuals are actually held to account, however, corruption will continue to be a significant stress on the formation of the new state.

Weak Ties to Local Communities

Perceptions of identity in South Sudan are complex. The near universal support for secession among South Sudanese during the independence referendum reflects a powerful unifying value throughout the new country. Moreover, a strong majority of citizens identify themselves as South Sudanese. Still, tribal affiliations remain very strong. Many South Sudanese retain higher levels of familiarity, respect, and confidence in their tribal leaders than in political officials.[11] In some places, this has been a source of tension between the new state and traditional authorities.

During the war, the SPLM/A instituted the practice of appointing civil/ military administrators to supervise tribal chiefs in liberated areas and report to SPLA zonal commanders. Some scholars argue this practice distorted traditional processes, militarized the chieftaincy structures, and strengthened the SPLM/A. Others maintain that in areas where civil/ military administrators and tribal chiefs had cooperative relationships, it helped to reduce violence. Nevertheless, it severely challenged the connection between citizens and their leaders by making chiefs accountable to a different set of interests (i.e., the SPLM/A) than those of citizens.

The SPLM/A never succeeded in developing a participatory civilian party structure with authentic grassroots mobilization and organization across communities and identity groups, such as women's and youth leagues, not least because the SPLM/A leadership ultimately did not make this a priority. While secretariats resembling civilian ministries predate the CPA negotiations, the main civilian function of the SPLM prior to the pre-independence interim period (2005-2011) was to coordinate access for humanitarian organizations to areas under its military control. Effectively, security concerns took precedence over civilian administration. This inability to separate politics from administration has continued into South Sudan's first years of independence, with the RSS leadership largely unable to separate party and government processes and structures. Decisionmaking remains centralized and top-down, with policy determined by the president of the RSS and the chairman of the SPLM—positions intentionally designed to be held by the same person.

Hence, while there are positive unifying values in South Sudan, there are powerful divisive forces, as well. These are deepest in regions of South Sudan with strong legacies of ethnic violence. Coupled with the youth of the population—of which the vast majority has known only war—and the abundance of small arms in circulation (both leftover from the war and newly provided as part of Khartoum's post-independence destabilization strategy), the propensity to resolve disagreements through violence remains very high.

State Formation and Stabilization Framework

Scholarship on fragile states has arrived at a number of important findings on violent conflict and how countries escape from it. As summarized by Bruce Jones and Molly Elgin-Cossart,

> We know that it is difficult to sustain an exit from conflict, but not impossible; that inclusive political settlements are important to peace; that building trust and confidence around the political settlement and in reformed institutions is vital to success. We also know this takes time—often decades.

> To put it plainly, violence occurs in contexts where institutional alternatives to violence are weak or nonexistent; weak institutions combined with a range of political, security and economic motivations (and

> *external pressures) creates the conditions for conflict*
> *and violence.*[12]

Hence a state becomes fragile and ultimately fails primarily due to an absence of accessible, trusted processes for managing competing interests nonviolently. Resilient states, meanwhile, cope with stresses through "a combination of capacity and resources, effective institutions and legitimacy, all of which are underpinned by political processes that mediate state-society relations."[13] While much attention on fragile states is given to the symptoms of fragility, namely high levels of violence, humanitarian crises, or conflict-triggering events, it is the quality, credibility, and accessibility of political processes that largely determine fragility or resilience. With only inchoate state institutions, weakened traditional and community authority structures, and rising levels of corruption within the RSS, South Sudan lacks these fundamental elements of stability.

In particular, states that successfully manage competing demands across groups in society have representative and inclusive political processes through which citizens can influence decisionmaking, channel concerns and opposition to policies, raise and resolve disputes, and hold leaders and institutions accountable. The more inclusive, participatory, and trusted these various processes are, the more legitimate, stable, and durable the political system will be.[15] As these trusted processes deepen, so too do the benefits they produce. Countries with pluralistic political processes and systems that distribute power widely and provide for the establishment of law and order tend to have inclusive economic institutions that create a level playing field where property rights are secured and investments in new technologies and skills are rewarded. In other words, political inclusivity not only reduces violence and instability but also contributes to development and growth.[16]

Stabilizing a nascent state such as South Sudan, then, requires transforming extractive or predatory political and economic norms into inclusive, accountable institutions to manage political contests nonviolently and provide a propitious environment for sustained economic growth. However, this does not come about merely by signing a negotiated peace agreement or by adopting a new constitution and holding an election, though each of those offer opportunities for engaging citizens and advancing reforms. Rather, societies arrive at a set of popularly supported political processes over time. In fragile situations, this can take a generation or more.

Trust is the bedrock on which such political processes are built. Trust must be cultivated between groups that have been divided by violence, between citizens and the state, and between the state and other key stakeholders whose support is needed for recovery. The level of cohesion and trust in a society "often defines the starting norms of cooperation, equity, transparency, and social goals. Societies that are more cohesive have greater consensus on the direction in which they want to go and the willingness to cooperate to get there."[17] Consequently, generating trust and cohesion, between both the state and society as well as across ethnic, cultural, linguistic, or other community divides, is essential to developing stable and viable state institutions.[18]

The 2011 World Development Report found that most states that escape cycles of violence initially developed "inclusive enough" coalitions of stakeholders to support national confidence building and institutional transformation. Such coalitions generate national support for fundamental reforms, cultivate trust between government and society, and promote outreach to community leaders to identify local priorities and deliver programs accordingly.[19] Over time, the constructive collaboration that emerges expands confidence in the state as well as its legitimacy. As increasingly broader segments of society are included in trusted processes, political institutions become more effective and resilient, creating a virtuous cycle.

Simply put, the health of the society is of paramount importance to the health of the state. Fragile societies breed fragile states, whereas durable, resilient states have rich and robust social networks that engender trust within and across different identity groups. "Nations with stronger social cohesion tend to be more stable, better off economically, less susceptible to crime and violence, and subject to lower levels of corruption."[20] Strengthening social cohesion through confidence-building measures that improve state-society relations is a first order priority, then. It is the foundation on which all state institutions must be built.

The 2011 World Development Report highlights institutions that deliver citizen security, justice, and jobs as vital priorities. Timely, visible results in these areas are most effective in helping states break cycles of insecurity and reduce the risk of relapse.[21] Partnering with other actors—community, civil society, private sector—can accelerate gains and further restore confidence in the state.

Citizens, moreover, will not consent to be governed by a regime if there are no meaningful and accessible avenues through which it can be challenged and reformed.[22] On the other hand, citizens are much more inclined to work through (as well as support and protect) a system that builds a track record of fairness and takes corrective actions when established rules have been broken. Developing systems of accountability to serve as checks and balances, particularly around the executive, help build confidence in the state and provide the basis for institutional reform.

The processes through which state and society engage one another form feedback loops that are crucial to the credibility and responsiveness of the state. These processes happen through a variety of state- and society-based mechanisms that collectively provide complementary rings of accountability and thereby generate confidence in the state (see Figure 4).[23] State-based accountability mechanisms include: constitutions, elections, legislatures, courts, political parties, subnational government, a merit-based civil service, and a professional security sector, among others. Society-based accountability mechanisms include: independent media and access to information, civil society, social capital, and external norms and standards.[24] The development of any particular cluster is less important than the density, or layering, of accountability mechanisms across the state and society. This creates a more stable, resilient system in which there are multiple levels of constraint on the executive.[26]

For many fragile or transitioning states, such accountability structures are weak or absent (see Figure 5). Typically, power is concentrated in the executive branch, which directs other branches of government. So extensive is the authority of the executive branch that it exerts control over even ostensibly independent entities like the media and private sector. Similarly, civil society is marginalized and unable to significantly engage in a dialogue with government or draw attention to citizen priorities. The state-building challenge for South Sudan, then, is to move from a context of executive branch dominance to one of layered accountability in which the executive is still in the center, but ringed by overlapping layers of state and society-based accountability mechanisms.

Building Trust and Accountability Processes in South Sudan

Unsurprisingly, most accountability institutions in South Sudan are in their embryonic stages. While establishing a new state poses a unique set of obstacles, it simultaneously creates opportunities to establish checks and balances that would be more difficult to introduce if entrenched, patronage-based, dysfunctional institutions were already in place. Unfortunately, rather than investing time and resources in such accountability-building processes in the early years of South Sudan's transformation, government policies have too often undermined them.

State-Based Accountability Mechanisms

Constitution. An interim constitution written by the SPLM was amended without serious review just before independence to serve as a transitional constitution. A participatory and thorough national review process intended to culminate in the adoption of a permanent constitution is scheduled to unfold before elections in 2015. The transitional constitution gives extraordinary powers to the president with almost no checks afforded to other branches of government. The president cannot be impeached. He can dismiss the national and state assemblies and remove the vice president and state governors from office, as well as any justice or judge. President Kiir exercised these powers in January and July 2013 when he removed two state governors and the vice president from office and dismissed his entire cabinet. The national review process is far behind schedule and almost entirely an elite exercise. The basic concept of a written constitution—providing the formal rules for how the state will function—is still not familiar to most South Sudanese.[27]

Elections. The first elections ever held throughout South Sudan took place prior to independence in 2010 as part of the CPA process, with contests at the national (then the united country of Sudan), regional (within the GoSS), and state levels. In the South, the elections were marred by intimidation and violence by the SPLM. The selection of SPLM candidates for office at the state and local levels was also highly controversial, with the party's headquarters overriding many state-level party nominations. Some election results were completely disregarded at the state level. With no judicial recourse or other accountability structures through which to challenge these outcomes, several disgruntled losers took up arms (e.g., David Yau Yau in Jonglei state). The next round of elections is slated for 2015, though no electoral calendar was mandated in the constitution and thus the date of the election is left entirely to the discretion of the ruling SPLM. In the absence of greater accountability for public office holders, these contests will remain zero-sum exercises over who gains control of public resources, potentially resulting in ever greater divisions and violence.

Legislature. The South Sudan National Legislative Assembly (NLA) is dominated by the SPLM, which holds more than 90 percent of its seats with the remainder held by 5 opposition parties. Most members are elected based on geographic constituencies, party lists, and a women's list. Some are appointed by the president. Legislation originates almost entirely from the executive, and the NLA exercises little independent oversight of the executive in the form of hearings, investigations, debates, or budget management. Most parliamentarians have infrequent contact with their constituents and were elected based on loyalty to the SPLM. The majority of the population resides in rural areas and is still largely unfamiliar with these new political institutions, their representatives, and how they relate to the use of state resources or the presidency.[28]

Political Parties. Opposition parties are very weak, in terms of both resources and capacity, and are regularly intimidated and harassed by SPLM-affiliated security agents. Several parties are led by former commanders of rebel factions who opposed the SPLM/A during the war, rendering them inherently suspect and dangerous in the eyes of the ruling party. Most retain loyal armed forces that can be mobilized to fight.

Reflective of its military origins, debate within the SPLM is not encouraged, dissent is not tolerated, and decisions emanate from the top. The SPLM as a party is virtually indistinguishable from the RSS and therefore does not advocate for higher standards of accountability or checks on government abuses of power. Internal leadership contests in preparation for elections in 2015 threaten to split the party, particularly between those loyal to President Salva Kiir and those to former Vice President Riek Machar. Such rifts also threaten to further politicize ethnicity. In July 2013, President Kiir, a Dinka, dismissed Vice President Riek Machar, a Nuer, and SPLM Secretary General Pagan Amum, a Shilluk.[29] Without internal SPLM reform to handle intraparty contests credibly and democratically, the potential for political instability and violence will grow.[30]

Courts. South Sudan lacks a functioning independent judiciary with the power to interpret laws and rule on the legality of executive actions, much less provide recourse to justice for citizens.[31] Laws are poorly disseminated throughout South Sudan and there is a confusing array of customary chiefs' courts, which are appointed by state ministries of local governments, and government courts, which fall under the judiciary. Government courts variously find their origins in British colonial structures, Khartoum's rule in garrison towns during the war, and attempts at SPLM/A administration during the war. Paradoxically, efforts to rationalize customary law to a written set of rules in order to achieve more clarity and uniformity may be inhibiting recourse to justice by eliminating some of the flexibility afforded by traditional processes.

Courts at all levels are vulnerable to bribery and are widely perceived to disadvantage the poor.[32] Estimates are that two-thirds of South Sudan's states still do not have any government courts, relying on scarce roving mobile courts for formal justice. Recourse to public defenders, particularly for death row inmates, remains rare.[33]

The lack of viable recourse options through the courts, consequently, may lead more citizens to seek alternative dispute resolution methods, including through violence. The perpetrators of this violence, many believe, are able "to kill innocent people, loot livestock, destroy property, abduct women and children and commit acts of sexual violence with impunity."[34] Increasing accountability for violent crimes through public prosecutions and trials, especially for rural populations, would help to ease the burden on political and military institutions of responding to intercommunal and politically motivated violence.

Subnational Government. The constitution and several laws authorize the decentralization of certain security and social services to state and local governments. State legislative assemblies and Councils of Traditional Authority Leaders (COTALs) are also provided for, though their respective purposes remain unclear. When austerity measures took effect in mid-2012 due to the loss of oil exports, moreover, transfers to subnational authorities were largely curtailed, cutting the salaries of teachers and other state and local civil servants. Elected state governors typically appoint county commissioners who oversee education, basic healthcare, and other services, despite constitutional requirements that commissioners also be elected. Citizens are widely critical of both this practice and of the president's power to unilaterally remove elected governors from office.[35] Nine of the ten state governors are members of the SPLM. President Kiir has removed two governors from office—Lakes state in January 2013 and Unity state in July 2013. While the president may appoint interim governors, the constitution requires special elections be held within 60 days to elect new governors. This requirement was not met in either case. In Lakes state, an SPLA Major General was appointed as the caretaker governor and has instituted a number of harsh and sweeping legal, institutional, and personnel changes that have generated extensive opposition.

Civil Service. The RSS inherited an urban-based civil service from Khartoum's administration of Juba and other garrison towns during the war. Consequently, the majority of South Sudanese who live beyond the country's few urban centers rarely interact with government personnel. Government jobs, meanwhile, have become a primary source of employment—and patronage—in South Sudan. Thus, not only is the civil service inaccessible but it also performs poorly. Adding to the complexity, South Sudanese widely support equal distribution of civil service jobs across ethnic groups as a key measure of how inclusive the government is. Furthermore, friction exists between younger, often more educated diaspora returning to support the new government and those who remained in South Sudan throughout the war.

Security Sector. Neither the SPLA nor the South Sudan National Police Service has achieved significant progress toward becoming professional, apolitical security services. Both are largely untrained, illiterate, and ill-equipped forces derived from various amalgamations of the SPLA and other armed groups that existed during the war.[36] Citizens widely perceive them to be sources of insecurity, not protection. Many senior officers have assumed a pernicious sense of entitlement following their role in the liberation struggle. This has resulted in land seizures, preferential contracts, government jobs, and other lucrative benefits.[37] The RSS has plans to demobilize 150,000 of the more than 300,000 soldiers on the SPLA payroll. In January 2013, President Kiir ordered an extensive overhaul of military and police leadership, retiring 35 general officers including all 6 deputies of the chief of general staff. While these moves were generally perceived as reigning in corrupt and overly entitled senior officers, and therefore popular, there was no legislative oversight of the nominations of senior officers to fill these positions.[38] In general, there are negligible channels for exchange, engagement, or consultation between citizens and the security services.

Society-Based Accountability Mechanisms

Independent Media and Access to Information. In spite of an increasing array of private media—radio stations, newspapers, and online news sites—independent information is rarely accessible in South Sudan, particularly on subjects relating to insecurity, corruption, or anything perceived as critical of the government.[39] Human rights organizations have documented increasingly frequent attacks, intimidation, and detentions of journalists by security agents, resulting in growing self-censorship by local media.[40] The brazen assassination of prominent newspaper columnist and frequent government critic Isaiah Ding Abraham Chan Awuol outside his home in December 2012 prompted domestic and international alarm.[41] No murder charges were brought in this case and attacks on the media have continued.

The government's intolerance of criticism and suppression of independent media undermine claims it makes of being accountable to the public and seriously damage its quest for legitimacy. Moreover, trustworthy and independent information is essential to mitigate conflict, counter corruption and other abuses, check and balance South Sudan's preponderant executive branch, and increase citizens' awareness of their rights and duties. Most South Sudanese view free speech as a fundamental right, an important demonstration of democracy, and an essential means of holding leaders accountable.[42] Building a cohesive national identity will be impossible without a genuine public debate on what it means to be South Sudanese, a conversation that must include rural communities as well as urban ones. To do so, more independent media providing greater access to information is required, especially in local languages on radio stations, which represent an indispensable information lifeline for many South Sudanese who live in remote rural areas.[43]

Civil Society. South Sudan's January 2011 referendum succeeded in no small measure due to government partnerships with civil society organizations to register voters, to inform the populous about the process, and then to observe the vote. The result was a rate of voter participation rare in countries with limited experience in electoral management. Three out of every four eligible South Sudanese cast ballots. Since independence, however, South Sudan's budding array of civil society groups—service delivery organizations, research centers, human rights advocates, and women's, youth, and professional associations—confront an increasingly unfavorable environment. The government and legislative assembly are perfunctory, suspicious, and defensive in their engagement with civil society groups. Moreover, most civil society organizations are heavily concentrated in Juba.

Civil society, nevertheless, offers important linkages to rural communities and opportunities to develop networks of trust across ethnic, geographic, religious, and other communal lines. For instance, a coalition of civil society organizations known as the Civil Society Resource Team on the Constitutional Review Process is conducting citizens' dialogues and civic education programs in all 10 states. The resulting input will be shared with the National Constitutional Review Commission.[44] Another group of local democracy organizations, the South Sudanese Network for Democracy and Elections, is arranging and facilitating meetings between parliamentarians and their constituents and then helping constituents follow up on the concerns they raised. In these ways, civil society is helping to provide the nexus for dialogue and negotiation between government and society.

Social Capital. Social cohesion in South Sudan is strongest at the local level where sense of community and belonging to tribe or subtribe generates the most social trust and willingness to cooperate. There is relatively little that extends this cohesion across ethnic groups and regions, however, outside of pride in becoming an independent nation and the shared experience of struggling for liberation from Khartoum. Moreover, deep trauma from and the legacy of intra-South fighting sustains intercommunal (and intracommunal) discord.

During the war, mission-run boarding schools provided one of the only civilian platforms for building social networks across ethnic groups and geographic regions. The churches' role in social service delivery throughout decades of war and colonial rule, moreover, has made them among the most trusted institutions across South Sudan. Leaders of the 12 main churches, which are united together under the South Sudan Council of Churches and represent more than 60 percent of the population,[45] are frequently called on to lead local peace and reconciliation processes. In April 2013, President Kiir appointed the archbishop of the Anglican Church and the archbishop emeritus of the Catholic Church to lead a national reconciliation process. Religious leaders also advocate against human rights abuses and corruption as well as conduct civic education, including on the national constitutional review process. The churches' popularity and credibility as an independent voice with the public makes them a trusted venue for facilitating engagement across ethnic divides. The churches are also a voice of conscience with the RSS, which renders the relationship with senior government and party leadership difficult at times. For their part, church leaders are wary of being perceived as too close to the government lest they lose the trust of their communities.

Outside of the churches, scarce platforms exist to create social bonds and networks across communal divides. Even South Sudan's few functioning universities confront communal tensions, sometimes leading to violence and disruptions of classes for long periods of time.[46] The SPLM and SPLA are the two broadest intercommunal networks in South Sudan. However, perceptions of Dinka domination of both institutions, the limited space for open debate within the party, and the challenges of integrating tribally based rebel militia groups into the SPLA[47] constrain their contribution to building social capital. Indeed, the SPLM's failure thus far to effectively link the grassroots to the national level may help to explain the renewed interest in holding regional conferences to discuss matters of local and national importance across the South's three historical regional blocs: Upper Nile (Jonglei, Unity, and Upper Nile states), Greater Equatoria (Western Equatoria, Eastern Equatoria, and Central Equatoria states), and Greater Bahr el Ghazal (Lakes, Warrap, Northern Bahr el Ghazal, and Western Bahr el Ghazal states). Such conferences were held in the latter two regions in 2013, organized by state and local political actors across state boundaries and outside of SPLM party structures.[48] The conferences have provided forums to debate federalism as a system of national governance and other issues of concern.

External. Prior to independence, donors were vital for providing humanitarian assistance to communities in the South, facilitating the CPA, and ensuring international support for South Sudan's referendum. Since independence, however, international actors have grown increasingly frustrated with the RSS, particularly the decisions to shut off oil production and occupy disputed oil fields on the border with Sudan in early 2012. Many external partners are also increasingly concerned about the scale of corruption, abuses of civil and political rights, and reports of human rights violations, including killings and torture, by state security forces. Donors, accordingly, were not forthcoming in providing funding or new support to the RSS during its time of austerity. Feeling somewhat abandoned and greatly misunderstood, the RSS has become increasingly resistant to foreign pressure and input, even from its closest partners (the United States, the United Kingdom, and Norway). This has complicated donor support to state-building efforts. Donor dialogue is most productive under the guise of the g7+ New Deal for Fragile States, of which South Sudan is one of the pilot countries. South Sudan is also now a member of the World Bank and the International Monetary Fund and is in the process of negotiating a credit facility with the Fund, which will bring with it external requirements for financial accountability. Verification of South Sudan's ability to meet the membership criteria for the East African Community, a major trading partner and export corridor, offers further opportunities to encourage the RSS to improve its standards of governance and development performance.

In short, South Sudan's mechanisms of state- and society-based accountability structures are limited. Government leaders have been

Loss of Oil Revenues

South Sudan is the most oil dependent country in the world. The RSS was severely stressed by the loss of 98 percent of government revenues between January 2012 and June 2013 due to a dispute with Sudan over oil pipeline transport fees. (South Sudan relies on oil pipelines through Sudan to Port Sudan for all its oil exports.) During this time, the government operated under an austerity budget, nearly exhausting its foreign currency reserves. In September 2012, Khartoum and Juba reached an agreement to resume oil flows through Sudan. However, implementation was blocked until additional unrelated demands by Khartoum over proxy rebel militia support were resolved in April 2013. Export of South Sudanese oil finally resumed in June 2013, though allegations of reciprocal support to proxy rebel groups continue.

The impact of the loss of oil revenues was felt most deeply in Juba, where the bulk of the national budget has been concentrated since the start of the interim period in 2005. According to the Sudd Institute, South Sudan's 10 states received only 16 percent of the national budget even before austerity measures took effect. The loss of oil exports caused cuts in civil servant salaries, reductions in block grants to states, and delays in development programs. Since 85 percent of the working population is engaged in non-wage work, chiefly subsistence-level agriculture, the impact at the household level outside of Juba and state capital cities was more limited than would otherwise be expected—further testament of the effective separation between the state and the rest of South Sudanese society.

slow to appreciate the immense value of such processes in building legitimacy and stabilizing an otherwise weak state. At times, leaders have actively resisted community mobilization, ignored popular grievances, and suppressed efforts to improve accountability. In the absence of more diverse state-society engagement and layered accountability mechanisms, political power and wealth will continue to coalesce around the SPLM and the executive branch at the expense of a disempowered, ill-informed, and fragmented citizenry.

Strengthening State-Society Relations in South Sudan

South Sudan is still in the early confidence-building stages of state development. The CPA and other subsequent transitional reforms have proved insufficient to foster badly needed trust and inclusivity, without which the state will never develop the legitimacy necessary to strengthen and expand its capacity to govern. Thus, overcoming this trust deficit and improving state-society relations must be an overriding concern of the leadership of South Sudan if the new nation is to realize durable peace, stability, and sustained development.

Drawing on the experience of other societies that have risen out of fragility, three critical tasks for improving state-society relations are essential: building inclusive-enough coalitions, expanding space for independent voices so as to enable national dialogue, and realizing tangible successes to demonstrate the state's responsiveness to citizen expectations.

Inclusive-Enough Coalitions

The state needs to make a more concerted and genuine effort to build collaborative partnerships beyond the class of elites who have dominated South Sudan's political future thus far. This partnership-building process must also transcend societal fault lines and engage youth. By identifying viable partners, mutually beneficial priorities, and complementary strengths, such a strategy would improve the RSS's engagements with local communities. Whether it involves matters of security, political processes, development needs, or other issues, the practice of building inclusive coalitions would make initiatives and reforms more viable, sustainable, and effective while fostering trust for future state-building efforts.

Most South Sudanese have minimal to no interaction with the government in Juba. Thus, inclusive coalition building will have to take place at the state and local level as well as through nongovernmental groups with inter-regional networks. The elections for state and substate political offices are particularly important. There must be participatory mechanisms for citizens and communities to influence the selection of candidates as well as the direct election of state governors and county commissioners (as opposed to appointments made in Juba or state capitals). Similarly, impartial avenues for candidates from any political party to seek recourse for election irregularities are needed. Likewise, the president's ability to dismiss elected officeholders at the national or subnational level should be explicitly limited. The composition of national and state assemblies should also be clarified in the permanent constitution to be based on geographic constituencies as opposed to party lists or presidential appointment. COTALs also hold great potential for channeling citizen concerns and priorities and demonstrating that the state is serious about inclusion and responsiveness to local voices.

South Sudan's ubiquitous and loosely networked churches are among the most trusted institutions in the country. Their respected mediators have made significant achievements in local peace and reconciliation efforts, such as the Wunlit Dinka-Nuer Covenant of 1999 that ended deadly bouts of intercommunal fighting. Partnering with churches on issues of local dispute resolution, civic education, or simply to improve intercommunal or state-society communication could foster enhanced trust in the state. More generally, by engaging with trusted nongovernmental and civil society organizations, the state can enhance its own political legitimacy.

Greater engagement with societal actors by the RSS would simultaneously diminish the justification for violence by communities that feel they have been excluded from the political process. Likewise, the RSS must recognize the difference between violence that is politically motivated (such as that carried out by rebel militia groups) and incidents that are resource related (protecting livestock from banditry or resolving disputes with neighboring communities over land, water, or other issues). While neither form is constructive, approaches to each should differ.

The RSS should engage directly with communities mobilizing merely for self-defense so as to jointly shape strategies that will provide consistent protection for property and legitimate economic activity (such as grazing and access to water). These engagements and operations should also extend to all communities and ethnic groups equitably. The extreme levels of violence in Jonglei state, for instance, will not come to an end so long as the Murle community feels targeted by the state while Dinka and Lou Nuer interests are more frequently protected.[49] At the very least, the security services must cease their often indiscriminate responses to violent actors as the high civilian casualties that result only further alienate communities.

Expanding Space for Independent Voices

Access to independent information is indispensable to establishing accountability mechanisms on which a stable, developmental state depends. Beyond actively cultivating coalitions and inclusivity, the state must protect space for citizens and communities to express themselves if the processes of a state-society dialogue are to gain traction. Drawing on the experience of other democratic transitions, a massive civic education and public outreach campaign is required to sensitize the population to key democratic values and principles such as:

- The responsibility of all citizens to participate in political and policy debates so that citizen preferences can be heard

◆ Tolerance for opposing points of view

◆ Freedom of speech, media, and assembly

◆ Equality before the law

◆ The inalienability of rights for minority groups and parties

◆ Protection of private property rights

In addition to state actors, this effort should enlist the participation of religious leaders, traditional authorities, civil society, the media, opposition political parties, and international partners. These groups have the trust of various constituencies in society and, collectively, can reach the largest percentage of citizens possible.

Rather than trying to monopolize state-society relations, the RSS and the SPLM should recognize independent civil society actors as representing authentic perspectives of citizens that can contribute to a stronger and more stable South Sudan. Harassing, intimidating, or otherwise inhibiting these voices sends exactly the opposite message—that the state does not want a genuine discussion with its citizens and intends to continue to dominate access to power and wealth. The outcome of such an approach is perpetual resistance and instability.

Media bills to protect freedom of speech should be passed and signed into law. Security services should be prohibited from persecuting the media, civil society, and international human rights monitors. Credible, independent investigations into all cases of intimidation and violence against journalists, human rights activists, and civil society leaders should be conducted and the results made public. The perpetrators should be tried publicly under due process of law. These are all immediate, consequential, and concrete signals that the government could send of its serious intent to become a government responsive to its citizens.

Since the challenge of building a national consciousness is as much a cultural exercise as it is a political one, efforts to foster a new South

Sudanese identity should complement reforms to protect and expand political and civil rights. South Sudan's heterogeneity provides deep reservoirs of culture that, if appreciated and respected for their diversity, can foster a new national identity. This process includes identifying, documenting, preserving, and celebrating the rich cultural heritage in South Sudan as well as its shared history of liberation struggle. Music competitions, national sports teams, and youth sports leagues could build linkages across communal groups. Widespread pride in South Sudanese runner Guor Marial, who competed under the International Olympic Committee's flag in the 2012 Olympic Games, was shared across ethnic and cultural divides in South Sudan. Preparing a national team to participate in the 2016 summer Olympics affords a forthcoming opportunity to further deepen national pride. The stories of Manute Bol and Luol Deng, two South Sudanese stars of the U.S. National Basketball Association, continue to inspire youths of all ethnic groups across South Sudan. Wrestling competitions hold deep traditional significance for some groups in South Sudan, providing an opportunity to bring historical traditions into the new national identity as well as foster healthy interaction and competition between communities.

Tangible Gains Responding to Citizen Priorities

Achieving modest improvements on key popular priorities is a tangible demonstration that the government has the interests of citizens at heart. Beyond the outcomes generated is the process adopted, for this signals how committed a government is to citizen participation and input—and ultimately accountability. Four strategic priorities integral to the state-building process provide focal points for generating confidence in the state so that vital institutional reforms in security, justice, and jobs can proceed.

National Constitutional Review. A national constitutional review process was to have been completed by January 2013, leading to a final, permanent constitution soon thereafter. The review process is considerably behind schedule, so much so that the transitional constitution had to be amended to extend the National Constitutional Review Commission (NCRC) mandate for an additional 2 years to December 2014. This raises serious questions about the adoption of a new permanent constitution before the current terms of the president and national assembly expire in July 2015.

More importantly, South Sudanese are frustrated not only by the delays but by how inaccessible and exclusive the review process has been. The composition of the NCRC is seen as highly politicized and dominated by the ruling SPLM party. Statements by some members of the NCRC questioning the need to consult illiterate citizens (the vast majority of the polity) have indicated to many people that the process will not be consultative or inclusive.[50]

A specific cause for concern was that the original composition of the NCRC largely excluded civil society members. President Kiir subsequently revised the composition to account for greater inclusion of civil society, though it is still dominated by SPLM politicians with no other political parties represented. The NCRC also does not seem to have plans for broad-based consultations across South Sudan, outside of the individual efforts of civil society members of the commission. Moreover, the constitution is slated to be ratified by the heavily SPLM-controlled parliament without being put to a popular referendum, despite the fact that surveys show a large majority favors such a course.

The national constitutional review process is an opportunity to educate citizens about what a constitution is and solicit views about what kind of government the people of South Sudan want. Instead, the path provided for in the transitional constitution—a permanent constitution drafted by the NCRC, reviewed by an appointed National Constitutional Conference, and then passed by the NLA for adoption—seems set to replicate the ruling party's vision for how they should govern the country. It also leaves the product forever open to serious legitimacy challenges. There is still time to make this process more inclusive, participatory, and transparent.[51] In addition to institutionalizing more consultative engagement with civil society and communities, the draft constitution should be put to a popular referendum to demonstrate societal commitment to this political course while significantly boosting the legitimacy of the new state. The independence referendum of 2011 was perhaps the most unifying and participatory experience in South Sudan, and so a constitutional referendum may be able to recapture and reinvigorate citizen participation in governance.

An open and legitimate constitutional review process represents the most significant opportunity to lay an enduring foundation for national unity. A closed and exclusive process, however, will result in extended political grievances and perceptions of injustice. It will also seriously call into question the state leadership's commitment to democracy.

National Reconciliation. Although not mandated in the CPA or the transitional constitution, the RSS announced in early 2013 an initiative for a national reconciliation process in recognition of the country's long history of intercommunal fighting and grievances. Delayed by early disagreements over the reconciliation committee's mandate and membership, a new national reconciliation committee primarily composed of church leaders was established in mid-2013. Archbishop Daniel Deng of the Episcopal Church of South Sudan chairs the process supported by Archbishop Emeritus, Paride Taban, of the Catholic Church.[52] The churches now have a significant opportunity to lead the country in a process of national healing.

A process of national reconciliation holds the potential to help drive progress toward security and justice, two critical sectors highlighted by the 2011 World Development Report as necessary for sustaining an exit from violence. The stakes are high, however, since a poorly managed process will provide further justification for violence to "address" grievances, while delegitimizing future initiatives to address intercommunal differences. Extensive public consultation and communication on why a process is necessary, how it should proceed, and what role state and nonstate actors will play will be critical to the success of the initiative. It is imperative that the process be apolitical and managed by independent and trusted nongovernmental institutions given the roles of many of the senior RSS leadership in the long history of South-South violence. Ensuring every community has an opportunity to air its grievances will be vital to the credibility of the process. The difficult question of whether and what forms of justice will be administered in response to the findings of the reconciliation dialogue comprises another significant challenge for the committee, political leadership, and society at large.

Beyond the formal process for national reconciliation, promoting a culture of tolerance among youth and community leaders should be priorities. Numerous grassroots and civil society initiatives have attempted to do this during and since the war. However, some have neglected to include youth actors most central to perpetuating specific conflict dynamics, such as with the Murle and Lou Nuer youth in Jonglei state.[53] Unless and until initiatives include stakeholders connected to these actors and familiar with their motives and interests, success in reversing the increasing reliance on violence is unlikely.

2015 Elections. The 2015 elections represent an inimitable opportunity to build confidence and foster citizen participation and the legitimization of a governance agenda.

The current terms of the president, state governors, and national and state assemblies expire in July 2015, suggesting that elections should take place in the first half of 2015. The transitional constitution does not make this explicit, however, and the delays in drafting the permanent constitution create uncertainty as to the timing of the next elections. Nevertheless, a National Electoral Commission has already been formed and is beginning preparations. Its independence from the

SPLM and RSS leadership and preparations for a free and fair contest are crucial for building trust in the next government and its ability to advance reforms and implement policy.

How national elections and internal SPLM candidacy issues are handled will go far in setting norms for future elections in South Sudan—and whether these contests will continue to be seen as winner-take-all competitions that heighten the likelihood of violence. Whether the losers in the SPLM chairmanship contest and the presidential election accept the results peacefully will impact profoundly on the state's quest for legitimacy and viability. A key consideration in the lead up to elections for both the SPLM and the RSS will be to guarantee protections and space for the losers in the political process after the elections.

More broadly, the 2015 electoral process is an opportunity for all office holders to engage sincerely with constituents to deepen state-society relations. A question remains, however, whether there will be sufficient layers of accountability from both state and society for political actors to accept nonviolent competitions for power and resources. While this accountability-building process is still in a nascent stage, if perceptions take hold that the electoral process is not managed equitably and transparently, then not only will the legitimacy-enhancing benefits of this process be lost but the probability of instability and violence in South Sudan will increase.

Connecting the Country through Roads and Radio. The three critical processes unfolding in the lead up to 2015—national constitutional review, national reconciliation, and preparations for national, state, and local elections—all require the free and regular flow of information to citizens in even the most remote parts of the country. South Sudan's sheer lack of physical infrastructure to enable the movement of people, goods, and services across the vast country, including during rainy seasons, will be a severe obstacle to every political, security, economic, and development objective. While some effort has been made to build the country's communications and transportation networks since 2005, roads and radio coverage must be extended to every region of South Sudan as quickly as possible. So long as communities remain cut off from each other and from the government—physically and through the exchange of information—insecurity and political exclusion will persist.

Conclusion

There is no substitute for the trust and social cohesion that is essential to stabilizing and strengthening fragile states. The state's political legitimacy to act on behalf of its citizens is even more fundamental than the state's ability to perform, although the two are clearly related. Building trust takes time. However, it is a matter of utmost urgency if state-society relations are to improve such that cycles of violence can be prevented and reversed.

In South Sudan, then, the focus must first be on building an inclusive political process. Internal and external stresses will fluctuate, but what will keep South Sudan mired in instability is the weakness of its state-society relations. Enhancing these relations should be the overarching priority for government and civil society leaders. Without it, institutions capable of dealing with conflict will not successfully emerge. An intensive focus on building trust and fostering social cohesion through bettering state-society relations is vital to reducing levels of ethnic violence and improving security, justice, and jobs. There is no path to peace and development in South Sudan without first establishing the foundation of the state.

Notes

[1] Jonah Leff, My Neighbour, My Enemy: Inter-tribal Violence in Jonglei, HSBA Issue Brief No. 21 (Geneva: Small Arms Survey, October 2012).

[2] Jok Madut Jok, Mapping the Sources of Conflict and Insecurity in South Sudan: Living in Fear under a Newly-Won Freedom, Special Report No. 1 (Juba: The Sudd Institute, January 12, 2013), 7.

[3] Leff.

[4] "South Sudan: Army Making Ethnic Conflict Worse," Human Rights Watch, July 19, 2013, available at <http://www.hrw.org/news/2013/07/19/south-sudan-army-making-ethnic-conflict-worse>.

[5] "Survey of South Sudan Public Opinion: April 24 to May 22, 2013," International Republican Institute (IRI), available at <http://www.iri.org/sites/default/files/2013%20July%2019%20Survey%20of%20South%20Sudan%20Public%20Opinion%2C%20April%2024-May%2022%2C%202013.pdf>.

[6] Leff.

[7] P.M. Holt and M.W. Daly, A History of the Sudan: From the Coming of Islam to the Present Day (Harlow, UK: Longman, 2000), 130.

[8] "USCR Country Report Sudan: Statistics on Refugees and Other Uprooted People, June 2001," U.S. Committee for Refugees, June 19, 2001, available at <http://reliefweb.int/report/central-african-republic/uscr-country-report-sudan-statistics-refugees-and-other-uprooted>.

[9] Jok, Mapping the Sources of Conflict, 2.

[10] Traci D. Cook, Leben Nelson Moro, and Onesimo Yabang Lo-Lujo, From a Transitional to a Permanent Constitution: Views of Men and Women in South Sudan on Constitution-Making (Washington, DC: National Democratic Institute, June 2013). Traci D. Cook and Leben Nelson Moro, Governing South Sudan: Opinions of South Sudanese on a Government That Can Meet Citizen Expectations (Washington, DC: National Democratic Institute, March 22, 2012). "Survey of South Sudan Public Opinion."

[11] "Survey of South Sudan Public Opinion," 30.

[12] Bruce Jones and Molly Elgin-Cossart, Development in the Shadow of Violence: A Knowledge Agenda for Policy (Ottawa: International Development Research Centre, November 2011), 3.

[13] Ibid.

[14] Stephen Brown and Jörn Grävingholt, From Power Struggles to Sustainable Peace: Understanding Political Settlements (Paris: Organization for Economic Cooperation and Development, 2011), 11.

[15] World Development Report 2011: Conflict, Security, and Development (Washington, DC: World Bank, 2011), 10.

[16] Daron Acemoglu and James A. Robinson, Why Nations Fail: The Origins of Power, Prosperity, and Poverty (New York: Crown Business, 2012).

[17] Joseph Siegle, "Building Democratic Accountability in Areas of Limited Statehood" (paper presented at the International Studies Association Annual Meeting,

"Power, Principles, and Participation in the Global Information Age," San Diego, California, April 1-4, 2012), 12, available at <http://africacenter.org/wp-content/uploads/2012/07/Accountability-in-Areas-of-Limited-Statehood.pdf>.

[18] *World Development Report* 2011, 11.

[19] Ibid., 12-13, 119.

[20] Joseph Siegle, "Social Networks and Democratic Transitions," *Developing Alternatives* 12, no. 1 (Fall 2008), 42.

[21] World Development Report 2011, 13.

[22] Siegle, 2012, 4.

[23] Ibid., 12.

[24] Ibid., 8-10.

[25] Joseph Siegle, "ICT and Accountability in Areas of Limited Statehood" in *Bits and Atoms*, eds. Steven Livingston and Gregor Walter-Drop (Oxford University Press, 2013).Ibid., 12-13.

[26] Ibid., 12-13.

[27] Cook, Moro, and Lo-Lujo, 9.

[28] Ibid., 43-45. "Survey of South Sudan Public Opinion," 34.

[29] "South Sudan's Kiir Moves to Take Down Machar & Amum, Khartoum Says Accords Unaffected," *Sudan Tribune*, July 23, 2013.

[30] *Politics and Transition in the New South Sudan*, Crisis Group Africa Report No. 172 (Brussels: International Crisis Group, April 2011). Abraham Awolich and Zacharia Diing Akol, *The SPLM Leadership Contest: An Opportunity for Change or a Crisis of Governance?* (Juba: The Sudd Institute, July 23, 2013).

[31] David K. Deng, *Challenges of Accountability: An Assessment of Dispute Resolution Processes in Rural South Sudan* (Juba: South Sudan Law Society, March 2013).

[32] Cherry Leonardi, Leben Nelson Moro, Martina Santschi, and Deborah H. Isser, *Local Justice in Southern Sudan*, Peaceworks Series No. 66 (Washington, DC: U.S. Institute of Peace, 2010), 5, 39.

[33] Author interview with South Sudan Law Society, June 2012.

[34] Leonardi, Moro, Santschi, and Isser, 1.

[35] Cook, Moro, and Lo-Lujo, 48, 51.

[36] John A. Snowden, *Work in Progress: Security Force Development in South Sudan through February 2012* (Geneva: Small Arms Survey, June 2012).

[37] Jok, *Mapping the Sources of Conflict*, 12-14.

[38] *A Brave Decision or Security and Constitutional Quagmire? The President's Recent Military and State Reform Orders*, Weekly Review (Juba: The Sudd Institute, January 25, 2013).

[39] "Freedom in the World 2013: South Sudan," Freedom House, available at <http://www.freedomhouse.org/report/freedom-world/2013/south-sudan>. "Press Must Be Able to Work Freely in South Sudan," Open Letter to President Salva Kiir Mayardit, Committee to Protect Journalists, May 22, 2013, available at <http://www.cpj.org/2013/05/press-must-be-able-to-work-freely-in-south-sudan.php>.

[40] "South Sudanese Media Forced into Self-Regulation by Security Services," *Sudan Tribune*, May 27, 2013.

[41] "South Sudan Police Investigate Killing of Political Commentator," *Sudan Tribune*, December 6, 2012.

[42] Cook, Moro, and Lo-Lujo, 20.

[43] "South Sudan Public Opinion Survey," 70.

[44] "Nimule Declaration by Civil Society Resource Team on the Constitutional Making Process," *Sudan Tribune*, May 22, 2013.

[45] According to the Pew Forum on Religion and Public Life, 60.5% of South Sudanese in 2010 were Christian, 6.2% were Muslim, and 32.9% practiced traditional religions. *The Global Religious Landscape: A Report on the Size and Distribution of the World's Major Religious Groups as of 2010*, Pew Forum on Religion & Public Life (Washington, DC: Pew Research Center, December 2012).

[46] "Juba University Closes Indefinitely as Inter-Tribal Violence Escalates," *Sudan Tribune*, March 28, 2012.

[47] Cyrus Samii, "Perils or Promise of Ethnic Integration? Evidence from a Hard Case in Burundi," *American Political Science Review* 107, no. 3 (August, 2013).

[48] Justice Deng Biong, "A Call to Discourage Regional Conferences in South Sudan," *Sudan Tribune*, June 1, 2013. Lual A. Deng, *Regional Conferences in South Sudan are Imperative*, The Weekly Review (Juba: The Sudd Institute, June 25, 2013).

[49] Jok, *Mapping the Sources of Conflict*, 4-5. Leff.

[50] Jok Madut Jok, *South Sudan: A Politics of Demise or a Vision for Progress?* The Weekly Review (Juba: The Sudd Institute, March 9, 2013).

[51] *My Mother Will Not Come to Juba: South Sudanese Debate the Making of the Constitution*, Juba University Lectures 2013 (London: Rift Valley Institute, 2013).

[52] *Peace and Reconciliation in South Sudan: A Conversation for Justice and Stability*, Special Report No. 2 (Juba: The Sudd Institute, June 7, 2013).

[53] Leff, 8.

About the Author

Kate Almquist Knopf is an independent consultant on African issues and global development policy. She served previously as Assistant Administrator for Africa and Mission Director for Sudan and South Sudan in the U.S. Agency for International Development. Ms. Knopf represented the U.S. Government to the international Assessment and Evaluation Commission charged with overseeing the implementation of the Comprehensive Peace Agreement between Sudan and South Sudan. She is an adjunct faculty member of the Africa Center for Strategic Studies. She can be contacted at kate.almquist@gmail.com.